Courageous Heroes of the American West

Davy Crockett

Courageous Hero of the Alamo

William R. Sanford and Carl R. Green

Enslow Publishers, Inc.
40 Industrial Road
Box 398
Berkeley Heights, NJ 07922
USA
http://www.enslow.com

Original edition published as *Davy Crockett: Defender of the Alamo* in 1996.

Library of Congress Cataloging-in-Publication Data

Sanford, William R. (William Reynolds), 1927–
Davy Crockett : courageous hero of the Alamo / William R. Sanford and Carl R. Green. — [Rev. ed.].
p. cm. — (Courageous heroes of the American West)
"Original edition published as Davy Crockett: Defender of the Alamo in 1996."
Includes bibliographical references and index.
Summary: "Explores the life of Davy Crockett, including his childhood on the frontier, his time as a scout and soldier, his political career, and his last heroic moments defending the Alamo"—Provided by publisher.
ISBN 978-0-7660-4005-2
1. Crockett, Davy, 1786–1836—Juvenile literature. 2. Pioneers—Tennessee—Biography—Juvenile literature. 3. Legislators—United States—Biography—Juvenile literature. 4. United States. Congress. House—Biography—Juvenile literature. 5. Alamo (San Antonio, Tex.)—Siege, 1836. I. Green, Carl R. II. Sanford, William R. (William Reynolds), 1927– Davy Crockett. III. Title.
F436.C95S22 2012
976.8'04092—dc23
[B]

2011037749

Future editions:
Paperback ISBN 978-1-4644-0086-5
ePUB ISBN 978-1-4645-0993-3
PDF ISBN 978-1-4646-0993-0

032012 Lake Book Manufacturing, Inc., Melrose Park, IL

Printed in the United States of America

10 9 8 7 6 5 4 3 2 1

To Our Readers: We have done our best to make sure all Internet addresses in this book were active and appropriate when we went to press. However, the author and the Publisher have no control over, and assume no liability for, the material available on those Internet sites or on other Web sites they may link to. Any comments or suggestions can be sent by e-mail to comments@enslow.com or to the address on the back cover.

♻ Enslow Publishers, Inc., is committed to printing our books on recycled paper. The paper in every book contains 10% to 30% post-consumer waste (PCW). The cover board on the outside of each book contains 100% PCW. Our goal is to do our part to help young people and the environment too!

Illustration Credits: Brent Moore / seemidTN.com, p. 11; © 2011 Clipart.com, a division of Getty Images, p. 16; *Davy Crockett*, © 1915, frontispiece, p. 39; Enslow Publishers, Inc., p. 21; © Enslow Publishers, Inc. / Paul Daly, p. 1; Everett Collection, p. 43; Library of Congress Prints and Photographs, pp. 7, 13, 26, 35; *Life of Col. David Crockett*, © 1860, frontispiece, p. 32; Mary Evans Picture Library / Mark Furness / Everett Collection, p. 30; Superstock / Everett Collection, pp. 8–9.

Cover Illustration: © Enslow Publishers, Inc. / Paul Daly.

Contents

Authors' Note

This book tells the true story of Davy Crockett. Davy was one of the American West's greatest heroes. In his day, he was known as an outstanding hunter, politician, storyteller, and soldier. His daring exploits were recorded in newspapers, magazines, and almanacs of the early 1800s. In more recent years, Davy has been featured in films, books, and a popular television series. You may be amazed to learn that one man could pack so much adventure into a single lifetime. If so, rest easy. All of the events described in this book actually happened.

Chapter 1

Victory or Death!

Dawn came to San Antonio soon after six o'clock on March 6, 1836. Inside the Alamo, the old mission turned fortress, weary Texans checked their guns. The men had been under siege for twelve long, bloody days.

Davy Crockett stood on the south wall. A tall man in a coonskin cap, Davy was America's best-known frontiersman. He was there to help Texas win its independence from Mexico. Freedom, Davy believed, was worth fighting for.

Eight hundred yards away, a red flag flew atop the San Fernando Church. Davy knew what the flag meant. General Antonio López de Santa Anna, Mexico's dictator, had vowed to take no prisoners. Victory, it seemed, lay within his grasp. The Texans were outnumbered, 2,400 to 183.

Colonel William Travis commanded the Alamo. On February 24, he had called on Texans to come to his aid. Thirty-two fighting men from Gonzales had slipped into the Alamo on March 1. No further help had come. James Fannin had four hundred men under arms at Goliad, but he was reluctant to risk the long march to San Antonio.

Commander-in-chief Sam Houston had long ago given the Alamo up for lost. In January, he had ordered Colonel Travis to blow up the fortress. Travis refused the order. He had prepared his men to fight to the end. His only course, he said, was "Victory or death!"

Santa Anna's troops advanced to the sound of bugles blowing the *deguello*. Like the red flag, the stirring music warned, "We take no prisoners."

A hail of rifle and cannon fire poured down on the attackers. Davy fired his long-barreled rifle with deadly accuracy. The enemy's muskets could not match Old Betsy's three-hundred-yard range. The first wave slowed and fell back. Santa Anna rallied his men, and they returned to the attack. Texans were dying, too. The survivors kept up a steady fire and managed to beat back the second assault.

Urged on by their relentless officers, the assault troops carried their ladders forward a third time.

Scores of Mexican soldiers died, but many reached the walls. Waves of soldiers in blue and white uniforms poured into the fortress. With no time to reload, Texans swung their rifles like clubs. The Mexicans pressed forward behind blood-stained bayonets.

Davy and a handful of Texans made a last stand in the barracks. They fought behind a wall of mattresses, chairs, and tables. One by one, the defenders fell, dead or wounded. Mexican reports of the battle told

In this painting, the outnumbered Texan defenders fire their weapons at the attacking soldiers inside the Alamo after the Mexicans had breached the fort's walls.

what happened next. Their shot bags empty, Davy and a few survivors laid down their arms. General Manuel Castrillon stepped forward. He pledged that the prisoners would not be harmed.

The sight of the prisoners sent Santa Anna into a rage. He tongue-lashed Castrillon for breaking his "no prisoners" order. Enrique de la Peña, one of Santa Anna's officers, caught sight of Davy Crockett. "Santa Anna," de la Peña wrote, "ordered [Crockett's] execution. . . . Several officers . . . thrust themselves forward . . . and with swords in hand, fell upon these . . . defenseless men just as a tiger leaps upon his prey."

The dictator's triumph would soon cost him dearly. Six weeks later, Sam Houston's troops engaged the Mexicans at San Jacinto. His fiery troops screamed, "Remember the Alamo!" as they routed Santa Anna's forces. Texas had won its war for independence.

Americans did not want to hear that Davy had died a prisoner. By the end of the month, a story that denied

Davy Crockett (center) raises Old Betsy as the Alamo's defenders make their last stand. Over the years, many stories of Davy's death have been told. The full details may never be known, but there is no doubt that he died fighting for freedom.

the Mexican report was making the rounds. "David Crockett," a writer claimed, "was found dcad with about twenty of the enemy with him and his rifle was broken to pieces."

In the long run, the details do not matter. What counts is that this great American hero died fighting to free Texas from Mexican rule. Those who knew him were not surprised. From childhood on, Davy Crockett had always been one of a kind.

Chapter 2

A Frontier Childhood

The Crocketts came to America from Ireland in the 1700s. Around 1776, David Crockett moved from North Carolina to the northeast corner of Tennessee. His son John fought in the Revolutionary War. After the war, John and his wife, Rebecca, started their own farm on Limestone Creek. Along with corn and hogs, the Crocketts raised a fine group of children. On August 17, 1786, their fifth son arrived. Rebecca and John named him David, after his grandfather.

John worked hard, but he never had much luck. In 1794, he built a small mill on Cove Creek. A flood washed the mill away that same year, but John did not quit. He made a fresh start by opening a tavern on the Virginia-Knoxville road. Each night, Davy listened as weary travelers spun tall tales before bedding down.

Soon the boy was telling stories of his own. The habit stayed with Davy for the rest of his life.

By 1798, John and Rebecca had six sons and three daughters. Money was scarce. Davy helped feed the family with the game he bagged in the woods. When the boy was twelve, John hired him out to work for Jacob Siler. Davy received $5 for tending Siler's cattle

Davy's father, John Crockett, opened a tavern on the Virginia-Knoxville road. Today, the Crockett Tavern Museum attracts tourists to the site in Morristown, Tennessee.

during the long journey to his farm in Virginia. When they arrived, Siler pressured Davy to stay with him. Unsure of his rights, the homesick boy agreed. Five weeks later, a friendly teamster helped Davy escape.

In 1799, John sent thirteen-year-old Davy to school. Before the week was out, Davy had a fight with the class bully. The punishment for fighting, he knew, was a whipping. Davy put off the beating by hiding in the woods each day. A week later, the teacher sent a note home, asking about Davy. John picked up a hickory stick and ordered his son back to school. Davy took off running. He outran his father—and kept on going.

Davy made his way back to Virginia. Doing farmwork paid twenty-five cents a day. After he had saved $7, he headed for Baltimore. There, Davy saw the sea for the first time. That same day, a sailing ship captain hired him as a cabin boy. Davy then went looking for teamster Adam Myers, who was holding his money. Myers put him off, saying he had spent the $7. Moved by Davy's tears, another teamster came to the boy's aid. Faced with a beating, Myers said he would repay the $7—when they reached Tennessee. Davy guessed that day would be a long time coming. Broke and discouraged, he gave up his dream of going to sea.

Davy Crockett first saw the sea when he traveled to Baltimore, Maryland, in 1800. This painting depicts Baltimore Harbor in the early nineteenth century.

For a time, Davy worked for a hatter. Eighteen months later, the man went broke. After that, odd jobs kept Davy fed and clothed. Finally, three years after running away from home, he walked into Crockett's Tavern. Hours passed before his sister Betsy recognized him. She gave him a big hug. His parents added their own warm welcome.

Davy went to work to pay John's bills. Six months of plowing fields and chopping wood paid off a $36 debt. A second six months retired a $40 obligation. His duty done, Davy stayed with the second farmer as a hired hand. John Kennedy was a kind man—and he had a pretty niece. The girl made Davy's heart "flutter like a duck in a puddle." He set out to court her, only to learn that she was engaged. Instead of pining away, Davy went back to school. If he was better educated, he reasoned, girls would like him better. After six months, he said he could “read a little” and “cypher [do arithmetic] some.”

Davy was now a lean five feet, ten inches tall, brown-haired and blue-eyed. Girls liked his good looks and his sense of humor. In 1805, he took out a license to marry Margaret Elder. At the last minute, the bride-to-be jilted him. Davy was certain he would never find another girl to love.

Nine months later, Polly Finley helped mend his heart. Davy met the red-haired girl at a country dance. A whirlwind courtship led to a wedding in 1806. The young couple set up housekeeping on a rented farm. Polly’s dowry of two cows and two calves helped stock the farm. Davy furnished the tiny cabin with a $15 credit at the general store.

Davy and Polly soon started a family. John Wesley Crockett arrived in 1807. William followed in 1809. In 1811, Davy purchased a five-acre farm in south-central Tennessee. Margaret was born there the next year. In 1813, the Crocketts moved to the Elk River country in southwestern Kentucky. Beyond Tennessee’s southern border, trouble was brewing.

Chapter 3

Campaigning With General Jackson

Davy was one of thousands of settlers who lived west of the Appalachians. The push into the wilderness led to frequent clashes with American Indians. Most of the settlers wanted the tribes to pack up and move west.

Two Shawnee brothers dug in their heels. Tecumseh and Prophet urged the tribes to drive out the settlers. The fiery Tecumseh said, "They seize your land. They corrupt your women. . . . Back whence they came, upon a trail of blood, they must be driven."

In Alabama, Tecumseh's words stirred up the Creek. Bands of warriors painted their war clubs scarlet and went on the warpath. Frightened settlers called them Red Sticks. In August 1813, a Red Stick raid surprised the guards at Fort Mims. More than five hundred men, women, and children died that day.

Tecumseh inspired his people to fight back against the settlers who were flooding into their territory and stealing their land.

News of the massacre alarmed Davy. He said he was going to join the local militia. Polly urged him not to leave her alone with three youngsters. Davy told her he could not let the Red Sticks scalp women and children. In late September, he signed on for ninety days with the Tennessee mounted militia.

Davy was picked to serve as a scout. He was out in the woods one day when he met a friendly Creek. The man said he had seen a Red Stick war party. Davy rode at a breakneck pace to bring the news to Colonel

John Coffee. To Davy's disgust, Coffee refused to act. Then Major John Gibson rode in with the same news. Convinced at last, Coffee sent a report to General Andrew Jackson. General Jackson's men searched in vain for the Red Sticks. The local Creek warrior, it turned out, had made up the story. He hoped the futile chase would keep the militia soldiers far away from his tribe's villages.

That November, Coffee's men took bloody revenge for Fort Mims. After a brief skirmish, the soldiers closed in on a Red Stick camp. Outgunned and outnumbered, the warriors offered to give up. As the soldiers approached, a woman killed a young officer with an arrow. The soldiers instantly riddled her with bullets. Then they set fire to her lodge. Forty-six Red Sticks had been hiding inside. They all died.

Davy went home on leave. After a visit with Polly, he returned to finish his enlistment. When he was released on Christmas Eve, the army paid him $65.59. To Davy, that was a small fortune. "I had done Indian fighting enough for one time," he said.

In September 1814, Davy again ignored Polly's pleas to stay. This time he signed up for a six-month tour of duty. "I wanted a small taste of British fighting," he said.

The United States had been at war with Great Britain since 1812. Third Sergeant Crockett was sent to Florida with the Tennessee Mounted Gunmen. At the time, Florida belonged to Spain. Even so, the English were using Pensacola as a naval base.

The Gunmen joined a force that easily captured the port. The soldiers arrived the day after the British withdrew. Davy wrote that the whiskey flowed freely that night. The rest of the campaign was tougher. Davy and his friends chased small bands of Seminole Indians through the swamps. When supplies ran short, Davy turned hunter. His deadeye shooting brought down deer and wild turkeys. Friendly Seminole traded corn for powder and shot.

In February 1815, Davy heard that Polly was sick. He returned home to find her burning with fever. He thought his heart would break when she died a few weeks later. The army called Davy back to duty, but he would not leave his children. He paid a young man to take his place. No one thought less of him, as the practice was legal at the time.

Later, when he ran for office, Davy described his army career in heroic terms. In truth, he played only a minor role in the War of 1812. He earned true military fame years later at the Alamo.

Chapter 4

A Fresh Start

By the time he was twenty-nine, Davy had filled out. He now carried 190 pounds on his tall, sturdy frame. His nose was sharp, and he had a pointed chin. He was proud of his ruddy cheeks, a sign of robust good health. Few could resist his charm and lively sense of humor. During the Creek War, Andrew Jackson said that Davy "kept the camp alive with his wit."

Davy needed a wife and his children needed a mother. A handsome young widow soon caught his eye. Elizabeth Patton had lost her husband in the Creek War. His death left her with a 200-acre farm, two young children, and $800 in cash. Elizabeth and Davy wed in the summer of 1815. The groom was now a man of substance. The owner of a farm that large was legally qualified to serve in the state legislature.

Davy had little reason to regret his choice. Elizabeth managed their affairs with thrift and common sense. Over the next six years, she also gave birth to three daughters and a son. Thanks in part to Elizabeth's modest fortune, Davy's neighbors gave him increased respect. In 1815, the men of Franklin County elected him a lieutenant of the militia.

As time passed, Davy became convinced that the region's climate was unhealthy. He and some friends rode south to look for a better place to live. While camping one night, the party's horses wandered off. Davy tracked the horses through creeks and bogs, but could not catch them. Worn out, he collapsed beside the trail. The chills and fever of malaria wracked his body. Luckily, some Creek hunters found him. Davy paid them to take him to a settler's cabin. With no doctor nearby, the settler's wife dosed him with a strong patent medicine. It was the woman's tender care, however, that pulled Davy through. The fever broke at last.

While Davy mended, one of his friends made his way home. The man did not know what had happened to Davy. He told Elizabeth that her husband was dead and buried. Weeks later, she thought she was seeing a ghost when Davy walked in the door. Davy did not

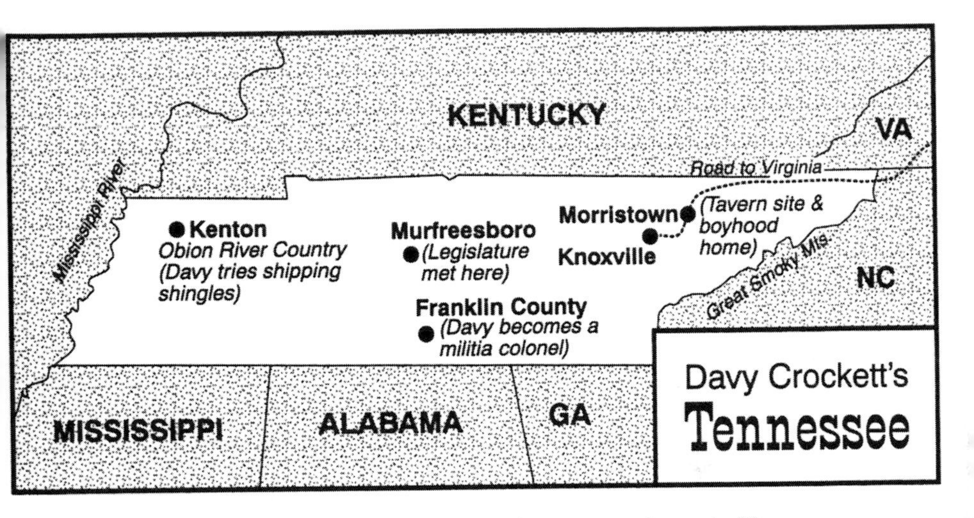

Davy Crockett and his family lived in many places in Tennessee, often moving westward to new and untamed regions after one of their business ventures failed. This map highlights some of the sites that played important roles in Davy Crockett's life.

blame her. "I was so pale, . . . my face looked like it had been half-soled with brown paper," he wrote.

Davy gave up on Alabama. Early in 1817, he leased his two farms and moved eighty miles northwest. Before long, a number of Crocketts and Pattons joined him at Shoal Creek, Tennessee. Davy's parents sold their tavern and moved there, too.

Davy and Elizabeth carved out a small business empire at Shoal Creek. After they cleared their land, they built a water-powered gristmill. Their neighbors paid them to grind their corn. Each day, Elizabeth turned about fourteen bushels of corn into cornmeal.

Much of the cornmeal went to Davy's distillery. His workers mixed the cornmeal with water and allowed it to ferment. A wood-fired still then turned the mash into whiskey.

A gunpowder factory was Davy's next project. Before long, his crew was turning out more than three tons of gunpowder a year. Davy sold the powder for thirty-seven cents a pound. A hunter could expect to get off ninety-six shots with a pound of Davy's reliable powder.

In the fall of 1818, Davy added public service to his workload. His first office was that of justice of the peace. While serving in that local office, he performed marriage ceremonies and sentenced thieves to be whipped. He also compiled the tax rolls. Later, Davy claimed that his judgments were always fair. No one, he bragged, ever appealed them.

Next came an even greater honor. The men of the Fifty-seventh Regiment of Militia elected Davy as their commandant. He took great pleasure in being called Colonel Crockett. Davy also found a new passion—running for political office.

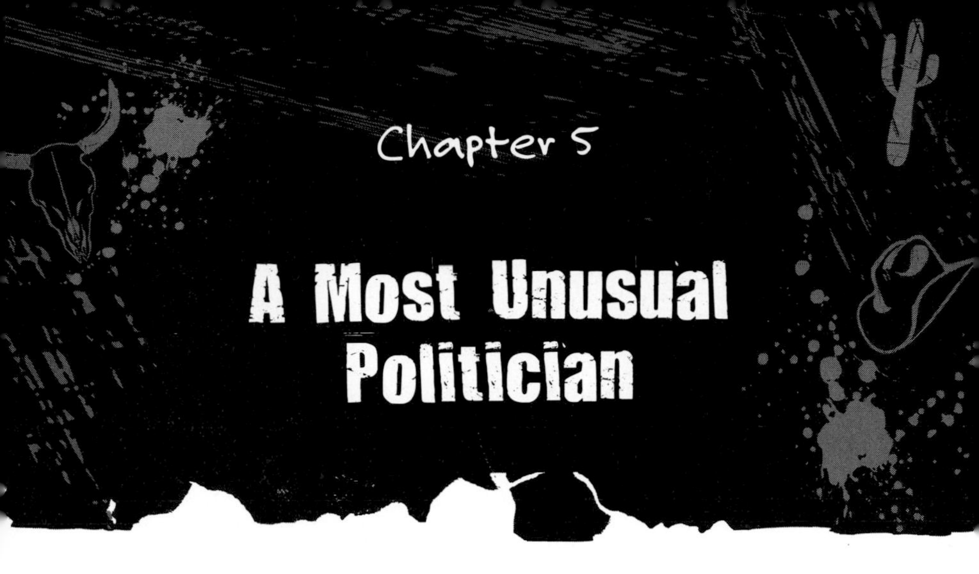

Chapter 5

A Most Unusual Politician

In June of 1821, Davy launched a campaign for the state legislature. The backwoods politician did not pretend to know much about state politics. He made up for his lack of experience by filling his speeches with funny stories. Standing on a stump and speaking to a crowd was a scary feeling. At times, Davy said, "I choked up as bad as if my mouth had been . . . cramm'd chock full of dry mush."

After he spoke, Davy often asked the crowd to join him for a drink. Wealthy landowners laughed at him. The poor farmers of his district laughed—and drank—with him. Davy was elected by a margin of 2 to 1.

The Tennessee legislature met at Murfreesboro in September. Davy quickly spoke up for the rights of poor farmers. Many were in danger of losing their farms. The problem had started when North Carolina issued warrants during the Revolution. At that time, Tennessee was part of North Carolina. These warrants gave veterans the right to claim federal lands in Tennessee. If a warrant holder filed for a piece of land, the farmer who was working it had to leave. Davy managed to slow this practice but could not stop it.

Back home, a fall flood swept away his mill and gunpowder plant. Davy rode home to inspect the damage. "[The mills] had cost me upwards of three thousand dollars," he wrote. "[This was] more than I was worth in the world." Davy and Elizabeth sold some of their land to pay their debts. They also had to give up their cabin. Elizabeth did not despair. "Just pay up as long as you have a bit's worth in the world," she told Davy. "Then . . . we will scuffle for more."

When the legislative session ended, Davy went looking for a new home. With his son John Wesley at his side, he headed west. He found what he wanted near the Obion River in the northwest corner of Tennessee. Eleven years earlier, an earthquake had toppled thousands of trees. Game thrived in the thick, tangled undergrowth. Father and son staked their claim in the spring of 1822. Then they cleared a field and planted a corn crop. The nearest neighbor was seven miles away.

In May, some supporters gave Davy a fine new rifle. This was the gun that later became famous as "Old Betsy." In July, Davy returned to the capital. He again fought the hated land warrants and backed aid to widows and children. When a bill to outlaw gambling came to a vote, Davy opposed it. He saw no harm in betting on cards, horses, or a shooting match.

By September, Davy was home again. To feed the family and to raise cash, he hunted bear, deer, and wolves. He killed one black bear, he swore, that weighed six hundred pounds. Each wolf he killed brought in a $3 bounty. Davy sold the deer hides and bearskins. He used the money to buy coffee, sugar, salt, and gunpowder.

Davy did not want to serve a second term. He was amazed, therefore, when a newspaper said that he was planning to run. The story was meant as a joke, but Davy took it to heart. He told Elizabeth he would go hunting for votes instead of skins.

During the campaign, Davy heard his opponent give the same speech day after day. One day, Davy asked to speak first. Then he stood up and recited his opponent's speech, word for word. The trick, Davy said, left the man "speechless."

After returning home from a legislative session, Davy Crockett went hunting to raise money for his family. Carrying his long-barreled hunting rifle, he bagged bears, deer, and wolves.

Davy also liked to describe the hunting shirt he claimed that he wore when he was wooing voters. One huge pocket held "a peck of tobacco." The other, he said, held a bottle of whiskey. The fictional shirt quickly became part of Davy's growing legend.

The voters gave Davy an easy victory. Back in Murfreesboro, he fought for his backwoods farmers. He voted to reduce taxes and to improve waterways. Although Davy worked hard at his job, he was often bored. If a debate droned on too long, he wandered off to find a tavern or a card game.

Davy's second term ended in October 1824. By then he had his sights set on a bigger job. He was thinking about running for Congress.

Chapter 6

A Bear Hunter Runs for Congress

Davy was not sure he should run for Congress. On his doubtful days, he moaned, "I knowed nothing about Congress matters."

The presidential election of 1824 helped him make up his mind. In a four-way race, Andrew Jackson fell short of a majority in the electoral college. With no clear winner, the House of Representatives had to step in. When the House voted, Henry Clay used his influence to elect John Quincy Adams as president.

Tennessee had voted for Jackson, who was a hero there. As outrage swept the state, Davy saw his chance. Adam Alexander was the man he had to beat in 1825. The wealthy planter had voted for Clay's high tariffs. To farmers, high tariffs meant much higher prices for imported goods.

The voters, candidate Crockett found, had to be courted. Alexander could afford to buy drinks after a rally. Davy campaigned with empty pockets. Legend says that he once traded a raccoon skin for a quart of whiskey. When the crowd asked for more, Davy stole the skin and sold it again. Later, he bragged that he swiped and resold the same skin ten times.

Davy lost the election by 267 votes. It was his bad luck that times were good. Cotton sold for twenty-five cents a pound that year. Alexander took the credit. He told farmers they could thank high tariffs for their fine year. Davy had to admit that his opponent knew a trick or two.

An old Disney song says that Davy "killed him a b'ar when he was only three." That is a tall tale, of course. What is true is that Davy grew up to be a master hunter. After the election, he took his dogs into the woods. Old Whirlwind, Grim, and Deathmaul treed many a bear for him. By the end of winter, Davy claimed to have killed 105 bears.

Once, on a cold, wet day, he stopped to build a fire. The flames scarcely warmed his hands. How could he keep from freezing? As Davy tells the story, he found a tree with a smooth trunk and climbed it. Then he locked his arms around the trunk and slid down.

The 1955 "Ballad of Davy Crockett" tells us that Davy killed a bear when he was "only three." While this tall tale has no truth to it, Davy was an excellent hunter. With his trusty hunting dogs and Old Betsy, he claimed to have killed 105 bears in one winter.

Rubbing against the tree "made the insides of my legs and arms feel mighty warm and good," he claimed.

The hunting was good, but the price of furs was falling. Davy turned to selling the narrow strips of wood, called staves, used to make barrels. He made plans to float some thirty thousand of these staves to New Orleans on two flatboats. Buyers there were paying good prices for staves and lumber. In January 1826, Davy and his crew sailed smoothly down the Obion River. It was later on the mighty Mississippi that Davy made a fatal error. The flatboats became difficult to steer after he ordered his men to lash them together. At Devil's Elbow, the boats hit a snag and broke apart. Davy was trapped in the cabin and almost drowned. His precious cargo floated on down the river.

The shipwreck cost Davy at least $100. It did not cost him his sense of humor, though. He said that when he got to Congress he would pass a new law. His bill would "prevent fools from going into the wood stave business."

With an eye on the voters, Davy worked to improve his image. When hands were needed to build a road, Davy volunteered. When men were needed for jury duty, the judge knew he could count on Davy. Elizabeth could have used him at home. She had to hire a man to help with the farmwork.

In 1827, Davy made a second run for Congress. Once again, Adam Alexander was the man to beat. William Arnold and John Cooke made it a four-way race. Cooke accused Davy of being a drunk and a gambler. Davy hit back. He told even bigger lies about Cooke. To clear his name, Cooke brought a witness to one of Davy's rallies. Davy was not rattled. He agreed that he had lied—but only because Cooke had started it. Both of us, he told a cheering crowd, are liars.

In this illustration, Davy Crockett gives a speech while running for political office. Davy was elected to Congress in 1827.

The other candidates ignored Davy. No one, they sneered, would vote for a crude backwoodsman. In August, Davy proved them wrong. He beat Alexander by more than two thousand votes. Colonel Davy Crockett was on his way to Congress!

Chapter 7

"I Can Walk Like an Ox, Run Like a Fox"

Davy's career in Congress nearly ended before it began. In October 1827, during his trip to Washington, he fell ill with a fever. A doctor treated the fever by bleeding the patient. The loss of blood kept Davy in bed for a month. When he did reach the capital, the fever returned. Congress was in session when he finally took his seat.

There was nothing modest about Davy Crockett. In a speech to the House of Representatives, he said, "I say, Mr. Speaker: I can outspeak any man on this floor and give him two hours start. I can outlook a panther, outstare a flash o'lightnin', tote a steamboat on my back, and play at rough and tumble with a lion. I can walk like an ox, run like a fox, spout like a volcano, and swallow a man whole if you butter his head and pin his ears back."

Davy paid $1 a day for room and board at Mrs. Ball's Boarding House. If he drank Mrs. Ball's whiskey, the price doubled to $2. Although he dressed in city clothes, Davy's manners marked him as a backwoodsman. Did he drink from his finger bowl at a state dinner? Davy denied the story. The public thought it was true—and loved him for it.

The slow pace in Congress made Davy restless. He sometimes drank and gambled when he should have been working. The record shows that he missed fifty-eight roll call votes in his first term. His pay of $8 a day did not cover his expenses. By the end of the session, Davy was $700 in debt.

Thomas Chilton was a fellow boarder at Mrs. Ball's. The congressman from Kentucky admired Davy. When his friend was mocked as a country bumpkin, Chilton turned ghostwriter. With his help, Davy's speeches became more polished. Chilton later served as his editor when Davy wrote his life story.

In Congress, Davy worked hard to pass the Tennessee Vacant Land Bill. The bill was as straightforward as Davy himself. If it passed, Tennessee would take title to all the vacant federal lands in the state. The next step would be to sell the land to poor farmers. The money raised would go to the schools.

A view of the United States Capitol around 1831. In Washington, D.C., Davy Crockett worked tirelessly to help poor farmers by supporting the Tennessee Vacant Land Bill. Unfortunately, the bill gained little support from other members in Congress.

As he studied the bill, Davy saw a problem. What if the state set the price too high? He asked Congressman James Polk and his committee to write safeguards into the bill. Polk, who also was from Tennessee, refused. Land speculators shaped the bill to their own needs.

In April 1828, Davy spoke in support of the bill. "The rich require but little legislation," he scolded. "We should, at least occasionally, legislate for the poor." The other side argued that giving away federal land would set a bad precedent. In the end, the bill never came to a vote.

Davy did not give up. He went back to Polk's committee. The government should give 160 acres to each settler in Tennessee's Western District, he said. The plan fell on deaf ears. The House adjourned in May without acting on the free land proposal.

During the summer, Davy moved his family to a new farm. He also began work on a new gristmill. This time he took the danger of flooding into account. Davy built his new mill well back from the river. Teams of horses turned the heavy grindstones.

In January 1829, Davy was back in Washington. He tried to add his free land amendment to the Public Lands Bill. His opponents worked just as hard to kill the plan. Some saw a threat to states' rights. Others worried that reduced land sales would take funding from the schools. After nine days of bitter debate, the House again set the bill aside.

Davy stayed in Washington to see Andrew Jackson sworn in as president. By late March, he was home again. Elizabeth was pleased to see that he had cut back on his drinking. His neighbors cheered him for sponsoring the Vacant Land Bill. Davy felt good about his chances for reelection.

Chapter 8

Wins and Losses

In August 1829, the voters gave Davy a second term. His victory did not please the Jackson camp. The president's friends saw Davy as a threat to their control of the state. If the land bill became law, Davy would be a bigger hero than ever.

Davy had rejoiced when Jackson won the White House. Now his ties to the president were weakening. Jackson's men went all out to defeat his land bill. Davy wrote that he still loved the president, despite the conflict. Then he added, "[I cannot] be compelled to love everyone who . . . pretends to rally around the Jackson standard."

With the bill going nowhere, Davy tried a new tactic. In December 1829, he arranged to have the bill moved to a special committee—with himself as chairman. The committee voted to allow settlers in

Tennessee's Western District to purchase up to two hundred acres. The price was set at twelve and a half cents an acre. The new bill failed, too. It finally did pass in 1841—long after Davy's death. His son John Wesley, who followed him to Congress, pushed it through.

By 1830, Davy's break with Jackson was complete. More than ever, he spoke out for the rights of the poor. In one battle, he took aim at West Point. Only the sons of the wealthy, he charged, went to the military academy. These "gentlemen," he said, were "too nice for hard service."

Congress ignored his half-truths. West Point stayed open. Davy also lost his fight to give pensions to Revolutionary War militiamen. The aging volunteers should receive the same treatment as army vets, he argued. The House buried the bill, 122 to 56.

In May, Davy stood up to defend the rights of American Indians. President Jackson wanted to force five southeastern tribes to move west. The plan was meant to clear the way for land-hungry farmers. Davy argued that the United States should honor treaties made with the tribes. He said, "If I should be the only member of that House who voted against the bill . . .

Although Davy Crockett had to dress in city clothes while serving in Congress, he was always an "honest woodsman" at heart. In his speeches, he drew on his adventurous early life to show how he would stand up to President Andrew Jackson.

I would still vote against it." The bill passed despite his protests.

The failure of the land bill, plus his break with Jackson, hurt Davy. His easy win in 1829 turned into an uphill struggle in 1831. Lawyer William Fitzgerald, a Jackson man, ran an ugly campaign. He charged that Davy was a drunk, a fraud, and a gambler. He said that Davy had cheated taxpayers by missing too many votes in the House. Davy vowed to punch "Little Fitz" if he told more lies.

At a rally in the town of Paris, Tennessee, Fitzgerald spoke first. When he repeated his charges, Davy jumped up and started toward him. The lawyer drew a pistol. He threatened to shoot Davy if he came closer.

Unsure for once of what to do, Davy went back to his seat. The news of the face-off spread like wildfire. Davy, the story went, had looked old and tired. In August, he lost a close race by 595 votes.

At forty-five, Davy did not feel old. During the next two years, he mended his political fences. By 1833, the voters were on his side again. A poor cotton crop had left farmers deeply in debt. Money was scarce, and banks had little cash to loan. In a close race, Davy regained his seat in Congress by 173 votes.

Davy pushed again for his land bill, but his old fire was missing. More than ever, he worked on his public image. In his speeches, he posed as the simple backwoodsman who had stood up to President Jackson. "Look at my neck," he wrote. "You will not find there any collar, with the engraving 'MY DOG. Andrew Jackson.'"

Back home, Davy's friends were worried. They warned that Jackson's Democratic Party might deny him a fourth term. Davy was riding too high to listen. Leaders in the Whig party were wining and dining him. There was talk of running "the honest woodsman" for president.

Chapter 9

"Be Always Sure You're Right"

The American people loved Davy's tall tales, and half believed them. If Davy said he could "grin" a raccoon out of a tree, few would doubt him. In 1834, with Thomas Chilton's help, Davy wrote his life story. The book retold Davy's adventures and blasted his foes. *Narrative of the Life of Davy Crockett of the State of Tennessee, Written by Himself*, became a best seller.

In the spring of 1834, Davy toured the major cities of the East. At Bunker Hill, he said he felt he was standing on holy ground. In Philadelphia, his fans gave him a fine new rifle. Davy named the gun Pretty Betsy. He described the trip in *An Account of Col. Crockett's Tour to the North and Down East*. That book, too, was a best seller.

The almanacs of the day printed weather and crop information. As Davy's fame grew, the almanacs increased sales by adding tall tales of his exploits. Did Davy cross the Mississippi on stilts? Did he fight the Battle of New Orleans from the back of an alligator? The Crockett almanacs swore he did.

Wooden-legged Adam Huntsman challenged Davy in the election of 1835. "Timber Toes" raked up all the old tales of Davy's drinking and gambling. Davy ignored the charges. He toured the district, telling stories and basking in the warmth of the crowds. To Davy's surprise, the old tactics did not work. He lost his seat by 252 votes. The Jackson camp, he protested, had paid $25 a head for Huntsman's winning votes.

During the campaign, Davy had made a promise. If elected, he said he would give the voters his best. If not, the voters "might all go to hell, and I would go to Texas." Davy was drawn by the lure of cheap land. It was a chance to pay off debts and make a new start.

Davy was as good as his word. He grabbed Old Betsy and set out for Texas. By the time he reached the Texas border, he was low on money. He solved that problem by swapping his watch for a cheaper one and $30. By then, his party had grown to sixteen or more "Crockett men." All had heard the same rumors. Texas would soon be fighting for its freedom from Mexico.

At each stop, Davy was hailed as a great hero. In Nacogdoches, he and his friends took an oath of loyalty to Texas. On February 6, 1836, the party reached San Antonio. At the Alamo, the garrison threw a *fandango* in Davy's honor. The dance was in full swing when a messenger rode in with a warning. The Mexican army was advancing toward San Antonio.

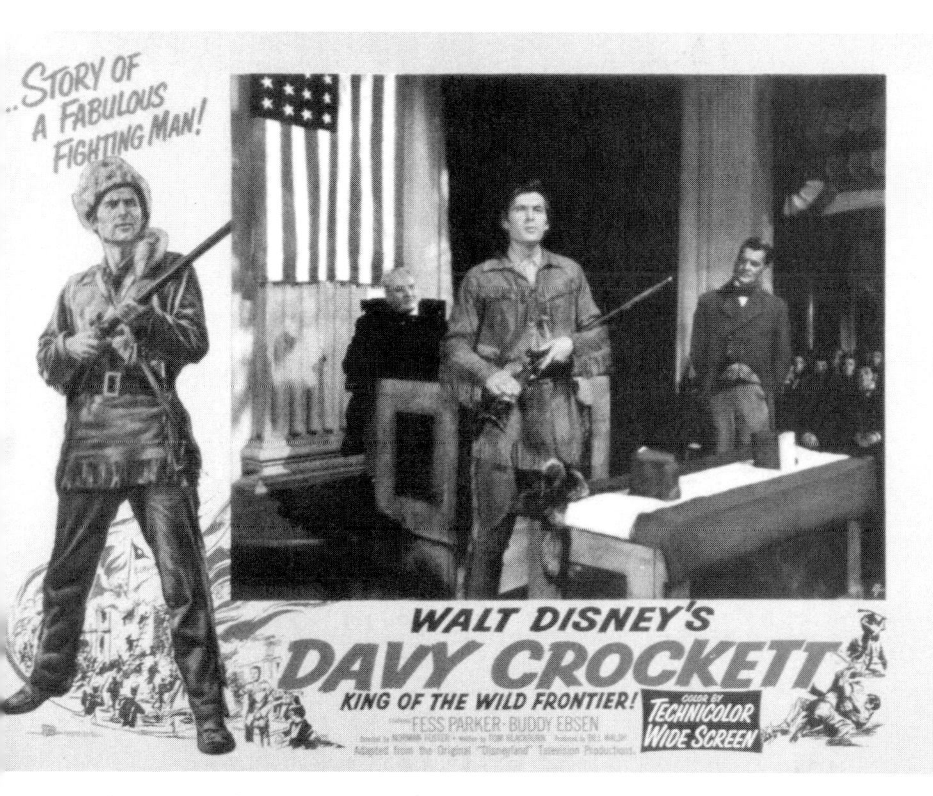

After Davy Crockett's death at the Alamo in 1836, his legend grew quickly. His life was portrayed in dime novels, plays, movies, and on television. This poster attracted moviegoers to the 1955 film, *Davy Crockett: King of the Wild Frontier*.

General Santa Anna laid siege to the Alamo on February 23. The Texans held his forces at bay for thirteen long, bloody days. Davy was everywhere, urging the men to do their duty. The final assault breached the walls on March 6. The defenders died to the last man.

History remembers Davy Crockett as a heroic defender of the Alamo. Since his death in 1836, his story has been told and retold in books, plays, and films. Even before his death, a play with a backwoods hero called Nimrod Wildfire had drawn big crowds. Nimrod was modeled after Davy. In 1910, a silent film glamorized Davy's death at the Alamo. In the 1950s, Disney brought him back to life in a popular television series. John Wayne portrayed Davy in the 1960 film, *The Alamo*.

"I can't understand [my fame]," Davy once wrote, " . . . therefore I put all the facts down, leaving the reader free to take his choice of them."

The real man, he might have added, is best summed up by his motto:

I have this rule for others when I'm dead,
Be always sure you're right—Then Go Ahead!

Glossary

Alamo—A former mission in San Antonio that was fortified by rebellious Texans in 1836.

almanac—A yearly publication that contains charts, tables, weather and crop information, and lists of useful data.

amendment—A change or addition to a proposed law.

bayonet—A long, sharp knife attached to the muzzle end of a rifle.

bleeding—An outmoded medical technique that treated illness by draining blood from a patient's veins.

bounty—A payment made to hunters who kill animals that prey on domestic livestock.

distillery—A plant where whiskey or other liquors are made from fruits and grains.

dowry—Money or property a bride brings to her husband as part of the marriage contract.

fandango—Spanish for a party with lively dancing.

flatboat—A raftlike boat with a cabin on the deck.

gristmill—A building equipped with large millstones for grinding grain into flour or meal.

justice of the peace—Official who presides over the lowest level of county courts.

legislature—A lawmaking body elected by the voters of a state or nation.

malaria—A disease transmitted by the bite of a female mosquito.

militia—Part-time soldiers who are called to duty in times of emergency.

mission—A group of buildings established by missionaries as the base for their efforts to bring religion and education to native peoples.

musket—A smoothbore, muzzle-loading shoulder gun.

patent medicine—A medicine that can be purchased without a prescription.

pensions—Monthly payments made to ex-soldiers and other retired workers.

precedent—An act or decision that is used as a guide for future decisions.

scouts—Skilled woodsmen who guide their own troops and keep watch on enemy forces.

session—The official period during which a legislature meets and conducts business.

speculator—Someone who engages in risky ventures in hopes of making a quick profit.

still—A covered metal container in which vapor from a boiling liquid is cooled and condensed.

tariff—A tax on goods imported into a country.

teamster—The driver of a team of horses or oxen.

Further Reading

Books

Beller, Susan Provost. *The Siege of the Alamo: Soldiering in the Texas Revolution.* Minneapolis, Minn.: Twenty-First Century Books, 2008.

Benge, Janet, and Geoff Benge. *Davy Crockett: Ever Westward.* Lynnwood, Wash.: Emerald Books, 2011.

Hasday, Judy L. *Davy Crockett.* New York: Chelsea House, 2010.

Stanley, George Edward. *Davy Crockett: Frontier Legend.* Sterling Publishing Co., 2008.

Wade, Mary Dodson. *David Crockett: Hero and Legend.* Houston, Tex.: Bright Sky Press, 2009.

Internet Addresses

The Alamo

<http://www.thealamo.org/main/index.php>

PBS: Remembering the Alamo—David "Davy" Crockett

<http://www.pbs.org/wgbh/amex/alamo/peopleevents/p_crockett.html>

Tennessee History for Kids: David Crockett

<http://www.tnhistoryforkids.org/people/david_crockett>

Index